LEONARDO DA VINCI.

77 Unpublished Stories

The Universal Genius

For all ages.
Nature, Animals and Short Fables.
Water, Fire, Earth, Air

III

Introduction:

Leonardo was not only the brilliant painter, sculptor, architect, scientist, musician known all over the world, but he was also a writer of fairy tales. Short stories, scattered in various manuscripts and writings in the last decade of the fifteenth century, when Leonardo worked at the court of Ludovico il Moro. Inspired by typical themes of classic fairy tales, Leonardo's stories are characterized by having as protagonists not so much large animals, men and divinities, but rather plants, objects and small animals ignored by ancient fables, such as the spider or the butterfly. The attribution of human characteristics to simple tools, plants or inanimate objects is also innovative, which raises the bold fire, the superb cedar or the arrogant razor to the protagonists. The relationship between man and Nature is the leitmotif of all fairy tales, which is articulated according to four main themes: the need to remain in one's own state, with the suggestion of remaining within the limits imposed by Nature; the presumption punished, with the condemnation of those who exceed these limits; the criticism of complaining and excess, with the punishment of those who want a condition different from their own ...

Leonardo da Vinci was not only the genius and innovator known for artistic works and futuristic machines. He was also a storyteller of fables and legends, full of wit and moral commitment. The true character of his stories is nature in its multiform elements: water, fire, earth, air. Animals have life, thought and even the gift of speech. This volume collects stories suitable for children and adults, for a first encounter with the greatest genius in history.
Translated to try to remain as faithful as possible to Leonardo's way of writing and thinking.

Age of reading: from 4 years.

Summary

The crab

A crab noticed that many small fish, instead of venturing into the river, preferred to wander carefully around a boulder. The water was as clear as air and the fish swam peacefully enjoying the shade and sun. The crab waited for the night, and when he was sure no one would see him, he hid under the boulder.

From that hiding place, like an ogre from his lair, he spied on the little fish and when they passed he caught and ate them. "It's not nice what you're doing" grumbled the boulder "Take advantage of me to kill these poor innocents." The crab didn't even listen. Happy *and content, he continued to fish for the little fish, finding them with a delicious flavour. But one day, suddenly, the flood came. The river swelled, hit the boulder with great force, which rolled into the river bed, crushing the crab under it.*

The spider and grapes
A spider, after observing the movement of insects for many days, noticed that the flies were crowding mainly on a bunch of grapes with large and very sweet berries. "I understand, he said. 'He therefore climbed to the top of the vine, and from there, with a thin thread, he lowered himself onto the bunch, installing himself in a cell hidden among the grapes. From that hiding place he began to attack, like a thief, the poor flies that were looking for food; and he killed many ones, because none of them suspected his presence. But in the meantime it was time for the grape harvest. The farmer arrived in the field, also collected that bunch and threw it into the tank, where it was immediately pressed together with the other bunches. Thus, grapes

*were the fatal trap for the deceiving spider,
which died along with the deceived flies.*

The net and the fish

*At the bottom of the sea hundreds of fish have
gathered. They were tired of brothers,
children, friends who continually fell between
the meshes of the nets that the fishermen
lowered every night. "The trouble is that the
networks have not seen. In the darkness of the
night, even the bottom of the sea loses its
contours. Impossible to get out of it ""
Nothing is impossible if we stick together! "It
was the anchovy, which above all had seen
thousands of relatives disappear.
"What do you mean?" the others asked "That,
if we are united, we will die happier? What
nonsense! If we fill the nets all together, we*

*will only make the fisherman happy! We are
so angry about it "*
*"It is precisely this anger that will serve for
our salvation" He had not finished speaking,
when the big net fallen in the night rose and
all the fish ended up in it "Don't despair",
urged the anchovy "," Together! Together we
swim against the tide. All together! "All the
fish in the net obeyed: the net was caught and
carried away by the fury of the fish*

<u>The fleas and the dog</u>

*WHICH BUSINESS AFTER A LOT OF
SWEAT, NOTHING FOUND.*

*A dog slept on a lambswool rug. One of her
fleas, attracted to the soft fur, thought:
"Ummm, what a good smell this wool has, so
soft and fluffy: it sure is a better place to have
fun. I'll stay away from the nails and teeth of
this little dog who can't stand me attacking*

him "Without thinking twice, she abandoned the dog and dived into the thick wool of the carpet, determined to reach the skin" It's a tiring undertaking: I didn't think it was so difficult to get to the root of the hair ". Despite the efforts, which he undertook after so much sweat, were in vain, the flea had to surrender: the animal's fur was thick and left no space to reach and stick to the skin. "It's useless for me to insist. It was better before!" She snorted in annoyance and decided to go back to where she was before. Surprise! While she was busy in the soft fur of the lamb, the dog had woken up and was already running away!

The repentant and embittered flea, after crying and lamenting, died of hunger.

<u>The oyster and the mouse</u>

*An oyster was found, along with other fish, in
the house of a fisherman who was not far
from the sea. "Here we all die!" he thought as
he watched his ailing comrades pant in the
net. He saw a mouse go by: "Hey, mouse!
help me, take me to the sea. I don't want to
die! "The mouse has decided to eat it and
wants to open it:" I'll do what you ask me, but
you have to open yourself, otherwise how can
I get you there? "*

*The oyster opened its shell showing its
delicious fruit. It was a moment: the mouse
jumped to bite her, but that, ZAC, closed up,
imprisoning her head. "Help, help ..." the
mouse cried and wiggled.*

The cat heard it and ate it.

The ant and the wheat bean

An ant has found a nice grain of wheat. "This is luck! It is the largest grain of wheat an ant has ever seen! "
As soon as he grabbed it, the wheat cried out imploring: "Ant please, let me have the pleasure of being born, let me taste the joy of life: I will make a hundred to reward you"
The ant satisfied her: she knew how to wait patiently and from that grain a large golden ear was born which generously rewarded her

The spider and the lock

A spider scouting the room saw a keyhole.
What an ideal retreat!
Sheltered and safe, he could have looked out without being seen, weaving his webs and nets. The spider, believing it would find rest in the keyhole, decided that this would be its lair: lined with so much iron that the hole looked like an impregnable fortress that made it feel extraordinarily strong.
He already dreamed of the threads he would weave and the ambushes he would make on unsuspecting prey.
But here's a key that rings, slipped into the keyhole and crushed it.

The filling stone

At the edge of a delightful grove close to a stone road, smoothed by the water of the stream, stood a beautiful and shiny stone, which fortunately enjoyed so much peace surrounded by a carpet of grass and flowers of a thousand colors. Despite so much beauty, the stone spent all its time looking at the road made of stones: "Who knows how it feels down there? Everything is beautiful here, but I feel isolated and alone. I could live there with my sisters. Look how many stones! I almost rush and roll among them "
Thus, pushed by the water, she managed to reach her fellow stones and concluded the much-desired journey between them.

But alas! What happened was not nice: the wheels of the wagons, the hooves of the horses, the feet of the travellers gave her no respite. Now he's rolled, now he's been beaten; it was also chipped, covered in mud and animal dung. In vain she looked up there, at the place from which she had left, among the flowering pleasures of her solitary and peaceful peace.

Too late!

This happens to those people who leave the quiet and lonely life, in nature and in peace. Come and live in cities, among peoples full of infinite evils

Paper and ink

"Give me a valid reason why you despise me so much?" the issue of ink seemed to fall on deaf ears.

The sheet of paper, proud of its whiteness , did not resign: "You are black, of an unbearable darkness! Every time you get close to me you smear me: Look! Look, I'm all stained! "Seeing the paper all stained by the dark neglect of the ink, he continued to complain. The ink, unable to bear any more, began to drop words and signs.

"Stop it, I hate the dark so much! My whiteness: take away my whiteness! "

"Paper, put away so much ingratitude: thanks to the words and signs, which, as you say, stain your whiteness, thanks to these ink stains, you can be preserved, preserved and appreciated. You become precious.

The monkey and the bird

It happened that a monkey in his solitary wandering saw a birds nest in the branches of a tree. Curious and happy with the discovery, she approached: many of them who knew how to fly fled frightened. Only one, the youngest, failed: the monkey full of joy stretched out his rough hands, took him and carried him to his lair.

How she looked at him! How he liked it! A real treasure! In love with that wad she began to kiss him and kissed him again. She kissed him and held him so ardently that she choked him.

This story is told for those who, in order not to punish their children, it happens badly, ends up killing them for too much love.

<u>Fishing and Walnut</u>

A peach tree did not bear fruit: the walnut that grew not far away produced a large quantity of fruit every year, many more than the peach tree produced.

"That walnut is really rich. I cannot resign myself to the idea of being inferior to him. My next bloom will surely be very abundant and I will do my best to overcome it "He thought about it a lot and did a lot: spring covered him with flowers that were fruitful as never before. The peach tree was laden with juicy fruits hanging from the branches .

But alas, the envious tree did not reflect on a fundamental fact: the weight of the peaches was not that of the nuts! The weight of said fruit threw it thinned out and broke on the flat ground.

<u>The butterfly and the lume</u>

One evening, shrouded in darkness, a colorful, wandering butterfly was chatting to itself when it saw a light shining in the distance. Intrigued by so much sparkle, she reached him immediately: how beautiful! Approaching the flame, she began to dance in graceful circles, mesmerized by so much wonder. Not content with admiring her, the butterfly took it into her head to do with her what it usually did with fragrant flowers: it took courage and after a lap, it passed over the flame, crossing it.

She found herself stunned at the foot of the lamp and realized to her amazement that her leg was missing and the tips of her wings were burned. "What happened to me? "SHe wondered, unable to find a reason. How was it possible that evil could come from such a beautiful thing? After regaining some strength, with a swing of the wings it started again. She pointed to the flame, crossed it and immediately fell, burned, into the oil that fed it - "Damn light "murmured the butterfly at the end of its life. "I thought I would find my happiness in you, and instead I found death. Now I cry in vain for my mad desire: I have known too late and at my expense, your dangerous nature. "" Poor butterfly, "replied the light. - So I do to those who don't know how to use me.

<u>The superb plant</u>

A beautiful plant, which grew luxuriantly and proud of its foliage, could not stand the fact that a straight, dry, old pole was planted next to it.

"Palo, you are on me too much and I don't like your proximity. Can't you go a little further? "the pole did not answer. Not happy, the plant turned to a hedge of dried plums that surrounded it:" I tell you too: "it is certainly not a good sight to see so many bushes next to me! "but she also didn't answer.

That superb tree, he did not understand that one holds it straight, the other protects it from dangerous company

The sparrow and the hare

A hare, while running in the meadow, was grabbed by the talons of an eagle, which wanted to give it only one bite. She was seen by a passing sparrow, who said to her, "Ah, what a distracted hare! You should have paid more attention before you started running in the meadow and now you will finish as you deserve. What happened to your famous speed? To your legs? ".

The sparrow had not finished the sentence that a sparrow hawk threw itself headlong at him and caught him. Now it was the turn of the hare, who replied: "Unfortunate, you thought you were giving me a life lesson, but now you cry for your fate."

<u>The superb crow and the peacock</u>

Swollen with vain pride, a raven picked up the fallen feathers of a peacock and adorned itself with them.

Then, despising his companions, he joined the beautiful flock of peacocks.

However, these suddenly tore the feathers from the bird and sent it to flight with blows of beak.

The battered crow set off in pain to return to his group.

But from this she was rejected and had to endure humiliation.

Then one of those he had previously despised said, "If you had been satisfied with us and with our origins and wanted to tolerate what nature had given you, you would not have heard this affront, nor would you be sad now for this rejection."

Peacock

She hoped to be back soon, but the days passed without him showing up. The farmyard animals were hungry and thirsty; even the rooster no longer crowed.

They all remained motionless, so as not to waste their strength, in the shade of a plant. Only the peacock, even that day, staggered on its paws, fanned out its large multicolored tail and started pacing back and forth.

"Mom , asked the lean hen to the hen "why does the peacock do the wheel every day?"

"Because he is vain, my daughter; and ambition is a vice that disappears only with death. "

<u>Lily</u>

A beautiful lily flower had grown on the green bank of the Ticino river. Tall and straight on the stem, the flower reflected its white petals in the water; and the water wanted to take it over.

Each wave that passed, carried with it the image of that white corolla, and transmitted its desire to the waves that had yet to get to see it.

Thus the whole river began to quiver, the waves became restless and fast; and not being able to grasp the lily, well planted in the ground and so high on the strong stem, they rushed furiously against the bank, until the flood dragged down the whole bank, together with the pure and solitary lily.

<u>The plant and the pole</u>

A plant, which grew luxuriantly raising its plume of tender leaves into the sky, could not stand, next to it, the presence of a straight, dry and old pole.

"Palo, you are on me too much. Couldn't you go further? "

The pole pretended not to hear and did not answer. Then the plant turned to the thorn hedge that surrounded it:

" Hedge ouldn't you go somewhere else? You bother me. "

The hedge pretended not to hear, and did not answer.

"Beautiful plant - then said a lizard, raising its head and looking at it from below - but can't you see that the pole makes you stand up? Don't you realize that the hedge protects you from bad company? "

Vitalba

In the shade of the hedge, the vitalba wrapped its green arms around the trunks and branches of the hawthorn. At the top he looked around and saw another hedge lining the other side of the road.

"How I'd like to get there," said vitalba. "That hedge is more beautiful and bigger than this."

And little by little she, stretching out her arms, got closer every day to the hedge in front of her. Eventually he caught up with her, tied himself to a branch and happily began to wrap himself around her. But shortly after, along that road, travelers passed, who suddenly found themselves in front of that branch of vitalba that blocked the road. Then, with their hands, they broke it, tore it from the hedge and threw it into the ditch.

The lion

The puppies hadn't opened their eyes yet. For three days they had been between the paws of the lioness mother, groping only for milk, numb to any call.

The lion, on the sidelines, watched them.

Suddenly he stood up and, shaking his beautiful mane, let out a powerful thundering roar.

The cubs immediately opened their eyes, while all the beasts of the savannah fled in terror.

And like the lion, which awakens its young with a very loud cry, so only praise awakens the dormant virtues of our children; by encouraging them to study with honor, it puts in flight what is not beautiful and what is not good.

The caterpillar

Still on a leaf the caterpillar looked around: who sang, who jumped, who ran, who flew; all the insects were in constant motion. He alone, poor fellow, had no voice, did not run and did not fly. With great effort he managed to move, but so slowly, that when he passed from one leaf to another he felt as if he had traveled the world.

Yet he envied no one. He knew he was a caterpillar and that caterpillars had to learn to spin a very fine slime in order to weave their little house with wonderful art. Therefore, with a lot of effort, he started his work.

In a short time the caterpillar found itself locked in a warm silk cocoon, isolated from the rest of the world.

"And now?" he wondered.

"Now wait," answered a voice. "Just a little more patience and you'll see".

At the right time the caterpillar woke up and was no longer a caterpillar. He emerged from the cocoon, with two beautiful wings, painted in bright colors, and immediately rose high into the sky.

<u>**The mole**</u>

A mole, underground, was walking through the long tunnels that his family had dug and cleared over many years of work. She paced back and forth, up, down into the cellars as if she had very good eyesight; instead, like all moles, she had very small eyes and poor vision.

*Eventually she slipped into an unknown
tunnel and continued walking.*

*"Stop," shouted a voice from downstairs.
"This tunnel leads out, it's dangerous!"*

*The mole, on the other hand, kept climbing
until it found itself in a mound of fresh earth.*

*It raised its muzzle and exploded, but the
sunlight, like the glare of lightning, killed it.*

*Even a lie, like the mole, can only live if it
remains hidden; as soon as it comes to light
to be noticed, it dies.*

<u>The lumerpa</u>

*A wonderful bird lives in the lonely mountains
of Asia. Its song is very sweet, its flight
majestic. Its body does not cast a shadow*

*because its feathers shine with so much light
that they equal that of the sun.*

*Even when dead this bird seems alive: in fact
its body does not become corrupted and its
luminous feathers continue to shine as when it
was alive.*

*However, if someone dares to detach a pen to
make it light, it goes out immediately.*

*This very rare bird is called lumerpa; and it is
similar to fame, which remains intact and
continues to shine even after death, and which
no one can usurp.*

The miller and the donkey

A man wanted to prove that he had already been in this world before, and to corroborate his claim he quoted the philosopher Pythagoras; but another, constantly interrupting him, did not allow him to finish the conversation.

Then the first said to the other:

"And as proof of having already been there, I remember that you, in the previous life, were a miller."

Then the other, feeling bitten by those words, replied:

"That's true. You're right. What you tell me now reminds me that it was you who brought the flour to my mill."

<u>A friar and the merchant</u>

In certain periods the friars minor use to make Lent and do not eat meat in their convents; but along the way, to live on alms, they are allowed to eat what is placed in front of them. Therefore, when a couple of these friars fell into a tavern in the company of a certain merchant, who, being at the same table, to which he was not brought, due to the poverty of the tavern, a small cooked chicken was served, so this A merchant, seeing that this is not much for him, he turned to those friars and said: "If I remember correctly, do not eat meat of any kind in your convents in those days". At which words the friars were forced, by their government, without further pleasantries, to say that this was the truth: therefore the merchant had a desire for him; and so the pullet was eaten, and the friars did their best.

Now, after this supper, these diners all three went away in company; and after some journey, having found a river of good width and depth, all three being on foot - the friars out of poverty and the other out of avarice -, it was necessary that one of the friars, being barefoot, carried this merchant on his shoulders: the monk took on such a man to cross the river.

For this it happened that, being himself a friar in the middle of the river, he still remembered his rule; and he stopped, for the use of San Cristofano, raised his head in the direction of what irritated him and said: "Tell me, do you have any dinars on you?". The trader replied that he could not go around without him? "" Alas! ", Said the friar," our rule prohibits that we cannot take money with us. "And immediately he threw it into the water. This thing, known by the merchant jokingly the insult already done to avenge, with pleasant laughter, peacefully, half red with shame, the revenge lasted.

<u>The privet and the blackbird</u>

A tall privet suddenly felt its long thin branches, full of black berries, violently move, as well as ravage its leaves and skin its tender bark with sharp claws and very painful beaks. It was a blackbird, which was eating its new fruit.

The privet then expressed all his regret for this attack and begged the blackbird not to deprive him of its leaves, because he was in great need of them. They were a defense against the hot, scorching summer rays.

The bird, therefore, did not spare the poor privet arrogant and rude words in response. He said to him: "Shut up, wild bush! Don't you know that nature made you produce these berries for my food? Don't you know, rascal, that next winter you will be nothing but food for the fire? "

The poor tree fell silent instantly, enduring everything with great patience and without crying. Meanwhile he began to weave his thin branches all around the peasant blackbird, to form a spider's web which, in short, imprisoned and deprived the arrogant bird of his freedom. Happy and content with his work, the tree then turned to the blackbird, saying, "Dear blackbird, I am still here without being consumed by the flame you were wishing for. At the moment I saw you first in a wicker prison that I fireplace. "

<u>Laurel, myrtle, pear</u>

Seeing the laurel and the myrtle cut the pear, they cried aloud: "Oh, where are you going?" Where is the pride you had when you had your ripe fruit? Now you won't shade us with your thick hair. "Then the pear replied:" I go with the farmer who cuts me, and he will take me to the shop of excellent sculptures, which will make me take the form of Jupiter God with his art, and I will be venerated in the temple and by men and worshiped instead of

*Jupiter, and you are preparing to be stripped
and peeled of your branches, which those
little men will use to build the places around
to honor me. "*

<u>Chestnut and fig</u>

*Seeing the chestnut the man on the fig tree,
who bent its branches in reverse, and from
them inspected the ripe fruits, and which he
placed in his open mouth, undoing them and
abandoning them with hard teeth, causing the
long branches to collapse and fear said, 'Oh
cool, how much less do you care about nature
than I do! See how in me I have strictly
ordered my sweet children, first dressed in a
thin shirt, on which the hard and striped skin
is placed, and not content to benefit myself so
much, that I have made them the strong
house, and on it I have founded sharp and
thick thorns, in what the hands of man cannot
harm me. "Then the fig tree began to laugh
together with its children, and the laughter*

stopped, it said:" Know that man is of such genius, that he knows you and touches you with poles and stones from the undergrowth, stretched between your branches, they make you poor in your fruits, and those who have fallen infest with their feet and stones, so that your fruits may come out torn and mutilated, thus piercing your armed house.
But I am diligently touched by hands, and not like you by sticks and stones. "

The butterfly and the candle flame

Not satisfied with the vain and vagabond parpaglione to be able to fly comfortably in the air, won by the delicious flame of the candle, he decided to fly inside; and his joyful movement caused sudden sadness; it is imperative that in that light the thin wings be consumed, and the miserable parpaglione, who fell abruptly at the foot of the candelabra, after much weeping and repentance, wiped the tears from his wet eyes and raised his face, said: "O false light, how many like me you must have, in the past, miserably deceived. Or yes, I wanted to see the light too, shouldn't I have confused the sun with the false light of the dirty sevo? "

<u>The walnut and the bell tower</u>

Finding the walnut carried by the crow on a high bell tower, and falling through a crack,

*it was released from its deadly beak, prayed
to the wall, for that grace which God had
given her for being so eminent and great and
so rich in beautiful bells and so honorable
sound and why he rescued her; since she had
not been able to fall under the green branches
of her old father, and be in the fat earth
covered with its falling leaves and not to
abandon it: he asked that she having been in
the proud beak of the proud crow, that he was
wrong, it, he wanted to end his life in the little
hole. At those words, the wall, moved with
compassion, was happy to receive her in the
place where she had fallen. And in a short
time the walnut began to open, and to take its
roots between the cracks in the stones, and
those to spread out, and to throw branches
from the holes in her cave; and they, in short,
rose above the building and swelled the
twisted roots, began to open the walls and
drive away the ancient stones of their old
places. Then the wall, belatedly and in vain,
mourned the cause of her damage and,
outdoors, ruined most of her parts.*

Willow, magpie and pumpkin seeds

The miserable willow, finding itself unable to enjoy the pleasure of seeing its thin branches make or bring to the desired size and straighten towards the sky - because of the vine and some plants that were close to it, it was always paralyzed, without branches and damaged - and gathers all the spirits within himself, and with them opens the doors to the imagination; and being in constant reflection, and seeking with it the universe of plants, with which they could connect, which did not need the help of his bonds; and, being somewhat in this extraordinary imagination, the pumpkin ran into his thoughts with an immediate assault; and all the branches have collapsed with great joy, she seems to have found them company for her desired purpose - she thought that she is more inclined to bind others than to be bound - and having made such a resolution, she raised her branches to the sky; he was expecting some friendly little bird, who had such mean desire.

In the midst of whom, seeing the wandering near him, he said: "O sweet bird, for that help, which in these days, since the morning, you have found in my branches, when the cruel and rapacious hungry hawk wanted you devoured; and for those rests which you have often made on me, when you were tired; and for those pleasures which you have already used in my branches, joking with your companions in your loves, I beg you to take the gourd and beg from which some of his seeds, give them to me, who will treat them as if I had generated my body and in the same way use all those words that are of similar persuasive intention to give you the seeds, you language teacher, does not need to be taught. And if you do, I am happy to receive your nest above the birth of my branches, together with your family, without paying the rent. "

Then the bird made and stopped a few flourishes with the willow, told the willow that

*it accepted, raised its tail and lowered its
head and threw itself from the branch,
returned its weight to the wings, and those
that beat on the fleeting air, now here , now
there, curiously with the rudder of his tail
straightening, he came to a pumpkin, and with
a nice greeting and a few good words, he
begged for the required seeds. And lead them
to the willow, she was received with joy; and
she scratched the ground near the willow a
little with her foot, with her beak, in a circle
or against it and planted some grains. That in
a short time, growing up, she began with the
growth and opening of her branches to
occupy all the branches of the willow, and
with her large leaves to adorn the beauty of
the sun and the sky. And, not so great,
following the pumpkins, he began, by
disconcerting weight, to pull the tops of the
tender branches towards the earth, with
terrible torture and discomfort of those. Then
trembling and in vain collapsing, to make
them fall by themselves, and in vain delirious
for many days in similar deception, because
the good and strong bond that such thoughts*

denied, seeing the wind pass, to whom it was recommended, and it blew hard. Then the old and turned stem of the willow broke into two parts to the root, and fell in two, he himself wept in vain, and he knew who was born to never have well.

<u>The flame and the candle</u>

The flames had already lasted for a month in the glass furnace and when they saw a candle approaching them in a beautiful and shiny candlestick, with great desire they forced themselves to approach it. In between which one left its natural course and pulled itself into an angry vow, where it fed, and left the opposite, holes of a small crack, to the candle that was near it, threw itself, and with supreme gluttony and greed that devouring, almost at the end led; and wanting to make amends for the prolongation of her life, she tried in vain to return to the furnace, from which she had left, because she was forced to die and fail together with the candle; whence in the end with weeping and repentance in annoying smoke she was converted, leaving all the sisters in splendid and long life and beauty.

<u>Wine and the Mohammedans</u>

Finding the wine, the divine grape liqueur, in a golden and rich cup, and on the table of Maumetto, and mounted in the groria of so much honor, he was immediately attacked by a contrary cogitation, saying to himself: "What Am I doing? What am I happy with? Do I not see myself close to death and do not go out of the golden abode of the cup, and enter the ugly and fetid caverns of the human body, and there I am transmuted from sweet smelling liquor into ugly sad urine And if not so much, that I still have to spend so much time in hideous receptacles with the other fetid and corrupt matter that has come out of the human guts? "He cried upside down to the sky, demanding revenge for so much damage, and what so much contempt it would now be put an end, that since that country produced the most beautiful and best grapes in the whole other world, fewer were not vinified. Then Jupiter caused Maumetto's flask of wine to raise his soul towards celabro and that so contaminated, that it made him mad, and gave birth to so many errors, that, returning to himself, he made the law that no Asian drink wine. And then the vines with its fruits were left free.

<u>The mouse and the weasel</u>

While the mouse was besieged in one of its houses by the weasel, which with continuous vigilance awaited its defeat, and for a small

*spiraculo looked at its great danger.
Meanwhile the cat arrived and immediately
took the weasel, and immediately devoured it.
Then the mouse, sacrificed to Jupiter some of
his hazelnuts, thanked him very much for his
devotion; and he came out of his busa to
possess the freedom already lost, of which
immediately, together with his life, he was
deprived of the claws and ferocious teeth of
the cat.*

The tongue and the teeth

*"Emorsa lingua dentibus graviter vulneratori
succensebat atque diuturni iam saporum
beneficii oblita, in quibus quidem exprimendis
et porrigendis ad linguam aetatem fere
omnem viresque contriverant, dentium
immodicam vicinitatem et superbiam
accusabat. Responderunt dentes : «Si tamen*

ab iniuria fuit alienus animus, condonasse nonne oportuit?"

The tongue accuses the teeth of pride, as they bite it by mistake, when they have spent their whole life in reverence. The characters are the same, while the themes are, instead, the collaboration between the elements and the condemnation, by Nature, for those who do not adapt and do not respect its laws.

The superb cedar

The cedar, proud of its beauty, doubts the plants that surround it, and towered in front of it, the wind then, not interrupting, threw it to the ground, thinning.

The ant and the millet seed

The ant found a grain of millet, the grain taken from it cried out: "If you make me so happy that I enjoy my desire to be born, I will make you a hundred of myself." and so it was done.

The dissatisfied vitalba

The white alga, not being happy in its hedge, began to cross the common road with its branches and clung to the opposite hedge; hence it was broken by travelers.

The donkey and the ice

When the donkey fell asleep on the ice of a deep lake, its heat melted it and the donkey under water, to its detriment, woke up and immediately drowned.

The humble snow

Finding very little snow attached to the top of a pebble, which was placed above the extreme height of a very high mountain, he gathered the fantasy within himself, began to reflect with this, and meanwhile said: "Now I cannot be judged haughty. and proud to have in me a small amount of snow, placed in such a high place, and to bear that as much snow as here to show me a little, is less than me? Surely my small amount does not deserve this height, because I can very well, as a testimony of my small figure, know what the sun did yesterday to my companions, who in a few hours from the sun had disintegrated; and this intervened for having placed themselves higher than was required of them. to the wrath of the sun, and lower myself, and find a comfortable seat to my parva amount. "And he threw himself down, and began to descend, turning from the high beaches to the other snow, when the more he sought a low place, the more its quantity à, so that, having finished its course on a hill, it found itself almost no smaller than the hill that supported it: and it was the last that was defeated by the sun. Dictation for those who humble themselves: they are exalted.

The impatient falcon

The hawk, unable to bear with patience the hiding place that the duck makes by escaping from it and entering under the water, wanted to continue like the one under water and, wetting the feathers, remained in the water, and the duck, going up the air, mocks the drowning hawk.

The spider and the hornet

The spider, wanting to catch the fly with its false net, was on top of those from the cruelly dead hornet.

The eagle and the owl

*One day, the Eagle and the Owl made peace
and exchanged an embrace,
one swore with the queen's word,
and the other swore with the word of barn owl,
who will never conspire to damage*

of their children.

- Do you know my children? asked the bird
dear to Minerva. - Not me.

- Now I'm afraid, if you don't know how to tell
them apart,
you can make a sad slaughter of it.
You adults, for what little I know,
like the gods above,
do not calculate the minus and the plus,
but do with mortals
as if they were boots.
Oh yes, poor me
if you eat them! ...
- Dude, now, if you want
that you don't touch a pen to your children,
introduce them to me or draw them to me.

- Davver? done right away.
They are beautiful and cute little birds,
which has no equal among birds.
If you see them, exclaim: "Here they are."
Keep in mind well
these signals and do that through you

the sad Parca does not enter my house -.

It hasn't been long
that the barn owl father has become,
and one day he was out shopping
the Eagle came and they were seen in the
dark
of a crevasse of a cave or of a wall
(Still do not know),
some offended-looking birds,
clumsy, mangy and gloomy and hoarse in
song,
- These are not our friend's children, -
he exclaims, - and well I can
eat them -. Yes, he said she, and the griffin,
who is not Pythagorean in his meals,
gnaws them all to the bone.

When the Owl returned from the countryside,
and he found none
his children but only sharp nails and beaks,
raise your desperate cries to heaven,
and anger and lightning against the killer
the gods prayed.

*But there were those who said to him: - O
barn owl,*
accused of your evils,
or the natural sense, which he always wants
that whoever looks like you makes him
beautiful and lovable
Better for you, if for your own sake, you
hadn't inflated the words..

<u>The envious peach tree</u>

*The perch, having envied the large quantity of
fruits seen making the neighbor's walnut,
decided to do the same, took it alone in such a
way that the weight of said fruits threw it
thinned and broken on the flat ground.*

The walnut and the wayfarers

The walnut that showed the richness of its fruit on a road to travelers, every man stoned it.

The branch of the walnut

Doing well: for the walnut branch, which is beaten and beaten only when it has brought its fruits to perfection, it denotes those who at the end of their famous works are struck by envy for different ways.

The fig and the elm

Standing the fig tree near the elm, and looking at its branches to be fruitless, and having the courage to keep the sun on its unripe figs, reproachfully told him, "Oh elm, you are not ashamed to stand in front of me. ? But wait until my children are ripe and you will see where you are. "Which children then ripened, when a squad of soldiers arrived, it was his own, towering his figs, all torn and branched and broken. Who then being so crippled in his limbs, the elm asked him saying, "Oh cool, how much better it was to be childless than to come in such a miserable state."

The thrushes and the owl

The thrushes greatly rejoiced, seeing that the man took the owl and took away his freedom, tying him with strong ties to his feet. This owl was therefore, by means of the mistletoe, the cause not to make the thrushes lose their freedom, but their own life.

Suitable for those lands, which rejoice in seeing their elders lose their freedom, through which they then lose help and remain tied to the power of their enemy, leaving their freedom and often their lives.

The vain and arrogant razor

One day coming out of the razor of that handle with which he sheaths himself and placed himself in the sun, he saw in his body the mirror of the sun: of which he took great glory, and turned with indirect thought, he began to say with himself:

"Will I go back to that shop I just left now?" Certainly not. Gods forbid, that such splendid

*beauty falls into such cowardice! What folly
would it be if you took me to shave the soapy
beards of rustic peasants and do such a vile
operation? Certainly not. I want to hide in
some hidden place and spend my life there
with a quiet rest. "*

*And so, hidden for several months, one day he
came back into the air, and came out of his
sheath, he saw himself made in the likeness of
a rusty saw, and his surface no longer stained
the bright sun, With vain vain repentance he
wept irreparable damage , saying:*

*"Or what was better to exercise with the
barber the lost cut of such thinness. Where is
the shiny surface? Of course the annoying
and ugly rust has consumed it."*

*The same happens in the minds, which in
exchange for exercise give themselves to
idleness, which, like the aforementioned
razor, loses its acute suctility and the rust of
ignorance spoils its shape.*

The discontented stone of his lonely life

A new uncovered water stone, of beautiful size, stood on a certain raised site, where a delightful grove ended on a stony road, in the company of herbs, various flowers of different colors adorned, and saw the great sum of the stones which were placed in the street below. He wanted to drop down there, saying to her, "What am I doing here with these herbs?" I want to live with these sisters of mine in company. "And having fallen among her desired companions, she ended her inconstant course; and she began to be trampled a little by the wheels of the chariots, by the feet of shod horses and travelers, to be in constant work; those who beat the vault, sometimes a piece would rise, when it was covered by the mud or the dung of some animal, and in vain it looked at the place from which it had started, in the place of solitary and peaceful peace.

This is what happens to those who in a solitary and contemplative life want to come to live in cities, among peoples full of infinite evils.

<u>The flint and the steel</u>

The stone, beaten by the fire, was greatly surprised and in a harsh voice said to him:

"What presumption makes you annoy me? Don't worry me, you caught me in exchange. I've never hurt anyone. "To which the acciarolo replied:" If you are patient, you will see that a wonderful fruit will come out of you. "At these words the stone, giving itself peace, patiently resisted against martyrdom

*and saw the birth of the wonderful fire, which
with its virtue he operated in infinite things.*

*Said for those who are frightened in the
principles of their studies, and then who
themselves have the power to command, and
patiently give continuous work to their
studies, things of marvelous demonstrations
are seen to be produced.*

The farmer and the vine

*Seeing the peasant the utility that resulted
from the vine, he gave it many sustenance to
support it at the top, and, taking the fruit, he
lifted the poles and dropped it, making fire of
his sustenance.*

The vine and the old tree

The vine, aged on the old tree, fell along with the ruin of the old tree, and it was from the sad company that it lacked with it.

The Torrent

The stream carried so much earth and stones in its bed that he was forced to change site.

The net and the fish

The net, used to catch fish, was caught and carried away by the fury of the fish.

The snowball

The more the snowball rolled down from the snow-capped mountains, the more it multiplied its size.

The willow

The willow, which due to its long germination, wanted to grow beyond any other plant, was still always paralyzed by keeping company with the vine, which was pruned every year.

The Penance of water

*Finding water in the superb sea, her element,
she felt the desire to rise above the air, and
comforted by the element of fire, which rose
in a thin vapor, seemed almost the subtlety of
air, and, mounted in high, it reached the
rarest and colder air, where it was
abandoned by the fire. And the small grains,
shrinking, already unite and become heavy,
where falling, the surface converts into flight,
and falls from the sky; from where then she
was drunk from the arid land, where she, long
imprisoned, did penance for her sin.*

__The flame and the candle__

*The light, fire above the candle, consuming if
consumed.*

The revenge of the wine

The wine consumed by the drunkard. The wine with the drinker takes revenge.

Fire and water

The fire contends for the water put into the pot, saying that the water does not deserve to be above the fire, king of the elements, and therefore by boiling it drives the water out of the pot; so that to honor them obedience goes down and smothers the fire.

The painter

The painter disputes and competes with nature.

<u>The knife</u>

The knife, accidental case, cuts the nails from man, natural case.

<u>The mirror and the queen</u>

The mirror shines strongly, keeping the queen mirrored inside, and after that, the mirror remains vile.

The birds and the Cerasta

Come and see! She called a little bird to her companion. - There are four tender vermicelli playing on a leaf! -
In fact, on the four sides of a leaf, there were four small vermicelli, which stood, wiggling and writhing.
That little bird could not resist the temptation to eat those worms, so tender and well fed they looked delicious, and so he rushed down to catch, peck, and devour them.
The other bird saw it point straight and determined towards the leaf, then heard it chirp desperately; and immediately he saw the ruffled feathers of his companion, his wings flapping with force and force in the void: the leaf gradually rolled up around its companion, until, under the leaf, the terrible Cerasta appeared.

*Cerasta is a viper, very fierce and ruthless.
She has her eyes on four small movable horns
and when she wants to feed she hides her
whole body under the leaves, except for those
four tiny croissants; and by moving them she
makes the birds believe that they are tasty
vermicelli, and when those poor, unsuspecting
feathered birds rush to get them, she Cerasta
immediately squeezes them and devours them.*

<u>Gratitude</u>

*That morning the two old hoopoes, a male
and a female, a pair of birds that had always
lived together, didn't really want to fly. They
no longer had strength. A veil before their
eyes prevented them from looking at the
world; the sky was clear, but they saw a kind
of white mist that confused them. They were
old and sick. The wing and tail feathers began
to grieve, lost color and light, withered like
dry branches and fell.*

*The two ùpupe thus decided not to move
anymore and to wait together for death,
which was not long in coming.
But their children came instead. Young and
strong ùpupe of the forest. The first, passed by
chance; he immediately realized that his
parents were swollen and sick, and
immediately set off in search of his brothers.
When they were all there, the eldest of them
said:
- We have received from our father and our
mother the wonderful gift of life; they
protected, nourished and nurtured us,
dedicating all their affection to us. Now they
are sick, they have become almost blind and
can no longer fly for food. Now it's up to us to
feed them and take care of them.
At these words without even a twitter,
everyone moved. Some began to build a new
nest, others went in search of insects, still
others left for the forest.
In a short time the nest was ready and the
parents were delicately placed there; to warm
them some children covered them with their
bodies like females do when they hatch their*

72

eggs; others fed them, others, with their beaks, cleaned them by removing the old and sad parched feathers.

Eventually, those who had gone into the forest to look for a healing leaf that could restore sight also returned. They chewed the healing leaf and with the juice of that leaf they medicated the parental dry and lifeless eyes. Then they waited patiently. Soon after, the father and mother opened their eyes, looked around and recognized all their children. Their love, their gratitude had healed them.

The testament of the eagle

An old golden eagle, who had lived alone on a very high rock for many years, felt that the hour of death was near. With a mighty cry from her he called out to her children who lived on the rocks below, and when they were

*all gathered around her, she looked at them
one by one and said:*

*I nurtured and raised you because, from an
early age, you were able to look at the sun. I
let your brothers die of hunger who could not
bear the sight of her. So you are worthy of
flying higher than all birds. Those who do not
want to die never come near your nest. All
animals must fear you and you will not harm
those who respect you, but you will let them
eat the leftovers of your prey.*
*Now I am about to leave you, but I will not
die here in my nest. I will fly high, as far as
my wings will take me; I will reach out
towards the sun as if I had to go to him. His
fiery rays will burn my old feathers, I will fall
to the earth, I will fall into the water.*
*But from that water, by a miracle, I will be
reborn again, rejuvenated, ready to start a
new existence. So is the nature of the eagles,
our destiny. -*
*Having said this, the golden eagle detached
itself from her: majestic and solemn, it
revolved around the rock where her children*

were; then, suddenly, she headed upward to
burn her tired wings in the sun.

<u>The Basilisk</u>

In distant Cyrenaica lives a very dangerous
animal called a Basilisk, it is a very small
animal. It is no longer than twelve fingers and
has a large, ridged white spot on its head that
looks like a diamond. Even a whistle is
enough for the dreaded Basilisk to scare away
any snake, even if it is much larger than him.
Instead of spiraling, like all snakes, the
basilisk runs fast and straight, lifting its torso
into the air. As if he were a proud and
powerful warrior.
It is a terrible and very poisonous animal.
One day a knight happened to return to his
castle after a grueling tournament, when
suddenly his horse went wild. He leaned over

to one side and began to neigh in terror: he had seen the terrible Basilisk. The knight, who had the spear in his hand, immediately struck the poisonous snake and killed it. But the Basilisk, before dying, barely had time to bite the knight's lance. Immediately the powerful venom of the reptile began to rise up the fibers of the stem, reached the hand of the rider, and the man and the horse died in an instant in terrible suffering.
At that moment another Basilisk arrived, which, unable to kill anyone, blew against the grass and the bushes: so that the grass and the bushes withered and dried up, and the stones crumbled like sand.

The pelican and the snake

When the pelican left to look for food, a snake, well hidden in the branches, began to move towards the nest.

The little ones slept peacefully.
The snake approached and with a devilish
glint in his eye the slaughter began. A
poisonous bite for each, and the poor boys
immediately went from sleep to death.
Satisfied, the snake returned to its hiding
place, to enjoy the return of the pelican.
In fact, shortly thereafter, the bird returned.
At the sight of that massacre she began to cry,
and his lament was so desperate that all the
inhabitants of the forest listened to him
moved.

What's the point of my life now without you? -
said the poor father looking at his sons killed.
- I want to die too, like you! -
And with his beak she started tearing her
chest, right above her heart. Blood gushed
from the wound, bathing the young men killed
by the snake.
But suddenly the pelican, now dying, began.
He was hot-blooded and revived his children;
his love had raised them. And then, happy, he
took his last breath and died.

The Macli

In far north Scandinavia long ago, there was a rather strange beast called Macli. It was shaped like a horse, but it was bigger. And it was different from the horse in that it had an extraordinarily long neck and ears.
Macli ate grass, but grazed backwards. Exactly, on the contrary. Because his upper lip was very long, so long that if he went forward, that lip would cover the grass and close his mouth.
Macli had his legs in one piece, so when he wanted to sleep, he was leaning against a tree.
He ran with incredible speed, swinging his powerful, long, straight legs forward.
The hunters failed to catch him. They had tried to chase him with the most determined steeds, they had tried to undermine him, with ambushes, at the pass, surrounding the places where he grazed, but to no avail.
Nothing! That weird grumpy beast was truly unattainable.

*One moonlit night, some hunters surprised
Macli in his sleep and with great amazement
they realized that he was sleeping standing up
because of those long legs that he could not
bend.
So, without being heard, they left.
The next morning they sawed up almost the
entire trunk of that plant and in the evening
they hid behind the nearby bushes.
Poor Macli, after sunset, returned to his usual
tree; he leaned back to sleep; the trunk
snapped, the beast fell, and the hunters
caught it.*

<u>The crocodile and the icnèumone</u>

*A crocodile shed many tears after killing a
man sleeping under a palm tree. -See-said an
Ichneumon to his son-the crocodile is a
hypocrite, now he cries and will soon devour
his victim.*

*Indeed, after a while, the crocodile quietly
began to eat its prey. After the meal he fell
asleep on the river bank, with his mouth open,
to allow a bird friend of his, called Trochylus,
to enter and peck at the leftovers left among
his idents.
Pleasantly teased by the diligent little bird,
the crocodile opens its powerful jaws even
more in its sleep.*

Then the icnèumone said to his son:

*Now be careful. This is how traitors are
killed. -
And, running, he rushed into the crocodile's
mouth and quickly slid down the throat. From
there he passed into his stomach, broke it with
his sharp teeth, then entered the intestine
doing the same.
The crocodile, awakened with a start, began
to roll on the ground in pain, screamed,
feeling his bowels being torn, until, torn by
the icnèumone, he lay on his stomach, dead
and dead*

The kite

A kite, which had made its nest on the top of a very tall pine, revolved in the sky with open wings, guided by the wind.

With his keen sight he could see the fish darting to the surface of the water in the mirror-like pond: but, even that day, he decided to leave his children fasting. But it wasn't selfishness or malice. No. the kite, in fact, when he returned to the nest, the hungry chicks opened their beaks as usual, but he pecked them hard on the ribs and angrily looked them in the eye.

"No, dear children, today I'm not giving you anything to eat," he said. - You're too fat. You are greedy. Know that the kite, our breed, is a bird that beats its wings little and must always look for the favorable or opposite course of the wind; if the wind reigns above, the kite must rise above; if the wind dominates below, the kite must descend below. But if the wind is not there, the kite must float upwards by dint of flapping its

*wings and, from up there, then glide slowly,
and then rise, with difficulty, and descend
again.*

*And those who are fat like you cannot, for
sure, and will risk starvation. So, that's why
I'm going to keep you fasting today too! For
your own good.*

<u>The caterpillar and virtue</u>

*And yet, there, standing on the palm of a leaf,
the tender caterpillar was there. The
vermicello with many and many feet looked
with its little eyes in every part and in every
where, and turned in his thoughts. There were
those who smiled, those who greeted, those
who sang, those who jumped, those who ran
everywhere and above all flew. Everything
was joyful around, everything was moving
and vibrating with happy life. Only he, poor*

caterpillar, could no longer move his body, he had never had a voice, nor could he move as fast as the others, but above all he did not know what it meant to fly. His every passage from one leaf to another seemed to him a long, tiring and endless journey.

Yet he envied no one. He knew he was a caterpillar and that caterpillars had to learn to spin a very fine slime in order to weave, with great skill, precious and wonderful, their little house. Therefore, with a lot of patience and dedication, he started his latest job.

In a short time the caterpillar, tired and slow, found himself closed in a bench, a warm silk cocoon, a chrysalis, very distant and isolated from the world.

"What do I do now?" he wondered.

"Now you must know how to wait, my sweet little bruchino" answered a secret and mysterious voice, sweet voice of a mother never known. "Just a little more patience and you will see and hear".

And the caterpillar waited, waited confidently for the prodigy of mother nature.

*Then it was his right moment, and without the
alarm sounding, the caterpillar opened its
eyes and felt that he was no longer a tired,
slow caterpillar. He felt something soft and
white that kept him warm, wrapped in a
tender embrace. He cut a hole in the cocoon
with his new razor-sharp paws, two large
loose light veils. And he went out into the
sunlight. He no longer had his thousand feet,
no longer had that bulky body, nor did he fall
heavily to the ground. Now he realized that he
had two large, light and beautiful wings, rich
in a thousand multicolored colors and
luminescent in the sun. As if by instinct, as
Mother Nature wanted, the new being flapped
its wings and immediately soared in the air,
high, high, in the infinite sky.
This is how virtue appears, light and majestic,
and if well patient takes care of everything
and rewards patience.*

The dragons and the ducks

In that swamp, all of a sudden, all the ducks took off: someone had warned them just in time, before the dragons attacked them.
In fact, from above they saw, on the shore, a large number of snakes: they all had a crest and large paws with claws.
The dragons decided to cross the swamp to look for food on the other side; but they couldn't swim.
Then they crossed and intertwined their long bodies with each other, arranged themselves like the cobweb of a net, forming a single surface that looked like a huge trap, and holding their heads above the water together they crossed the swamp as on a prodigious raft .

"You see it?" shouted the older duck to his companions. "See what can be done by being united?" One for all and all for one!

<u>The spider and the bee</u>

One cool spring morning a worker bee went into a lush meadow flitting from flower to flower, looking for pollen. Suddenly, emerging from the corolla of a bluebell, she ended up trapped in a spider's web. Hidden behind a large fig leaf, the spider rejoiced and ran for its prey.
- You're a traitor! cried the bee. - Set your own traps to kill those who work! -
The spider came even closer and the bee, turning around, tried to sting it by pulling out the long and dangerous sting from the abdomen.
But the spider dodged him just in time and jumping on top of the bee told her holding her tight:

- Bee, but by what right do you have the courage to judge me? - You are like deception and fraud: you have honey in your mouth, but from behind you carry the poison with your sting.

<u>The Cranes</u>

A famous king was known for his wisdom and goodness. But alas, the envy of other kings had created around him many enemies, murderous, cruel and merciless. The cranes, his faithful and loyal guards forever, were worried about him. It was the night that bothered the most, especially when the defenses seemed weaker in the dark and enemies could sneak into the palace.
- What to do? The cranes were wondering. - The soldiers, instead of guarding, fall asleep; dogs, always on the hunt and always tired, cannot be relied upon. So, it is up to us, the

faithful cranes, to guard the palace and let our king sleep peacefully and safely.

And so the faithful cranes decided to transform themselves into sentries: they divided into groups, and distributed the various guards in groups, assigning each crane an area around the castle.

The largest group stretched along the large lawn that surrounded the palace where the king stayed with his loved ones; another group stood before the numerous entrance doors; a third finally decided to settle in the king's chamber to watch over him.

- What if we go to sleep? Some have asked.

- Against sleep - answered the older crane - we will all take a stone from the pond, we will hold it tightly with one foot, which we will hold up when we are still. If any of us fell asleep, the stone would fall to the ground and with its sound the alarm would come.

Since that day, the cranes, standing on one leg, have guarded the king. And no one has dropped his stone yet.

The Asp and the Icneumon

The asp is a very dangerous snake due to its deadly venom. There is no other remedy for the asp bite than to cut off the bitten parts immediately. However, this pestiferous animal has such a desire for company that it always moves with someone of its kind, male or female.

If, unfortunately, one of the two is killed, the other, with incredible speed, pursues the murderer: from that moment on he has only one purpose, to avenge his partner, and out of thirst for revenge he overcomes all adversities. If the killer is a soldier, the asp goes through the army without hurting anyone until it finds the culprit; there is no obstacle that can stop him, he overcomes every difficulty and only those who flee very quickly escape him or those who throw themselves into a stream.

He has sunken eyes and large ears; more than sight, it is the very fine hearing that helps him move.

*Like any animal, the terrible asp has its
deadly enemy: it is a mouse, a large mouse
that lives on the banks of the Nile River in
Egypt, which is called Ichneumon.
When it sees an asp near its lair, the
ichneumon runs to the river bank and dives
into the mud. But it's not out of fear or to hide
from the asp's sight. No. After being
completely immersed in the mud, the
Ichneumon resurfaces and the hot African sun
dries the mud on him. As soon as the mud
hardens and dries, the ichneumon plunges
back into the mud leaving the little head out,
then re-emerges and again from the hot
African sun which makes the mud dry on
itself, on top of the other dry mud, and then
continues again, dries up, and again plunges
into the mud. Thus, one on top of the other,
formed by the mud and the sun, three or four
layers of dry mud, which become hard as a
bronze armor.
At that point the ichneumon faces the asp with
his head held high and, like a hero in battle,
resists his attacks, waiting for the right
moment for the final attack. When the snake*

*opens its enormous jaws to kill the ichneumon
with its teeth full of venom, the mouse, with a
quick leap, leaps in up to the throat, and
stands there, right in the middle of the Aspis
throat and suffocates it.*

<u>The Phoenix</u>

*Flying and flying, floating in the warm air
between the desert and the sea, the phoenix, a
mighty and extraordinarily strong eagle, saw
in the distance the fire of a large camp, it
must have been an unknown tribe. It was then
that the Phoenix understood that the time of
the great test had finally arrived.
She had to have faith, she had to surrender
confidently and calmly to her fate.
The fate of a timeless time, where the
beginning did not have an end. Where it all
happened without a purpose, it just happened.
The Phoenix soared in the air solemnly and
decisively, with wings firm, strong and*

outstretched, and she climbed up beyond the clouds, then closed her eyes and with great rotations began her mighty descent.

She was the largest of all known eagles in the world, the most beautiful, for her rich and vivid plumage of a thousand colors.

When he was over her fire he felt her flame brush her feathers and, faithful to herself and to her fate marked by her, she let herself fall into the flames.

But when the fire went out, a small blue flame was released from the ash pile; she floated in the air, free, and rose, opening as if she had wings.

And the wings opened almost indefinitely: it was the phoenix that regained life, breath, light and was reborn from its ashes to live in the sky for another five hundred years.

Always like this: it was her task: to die on fire and be rebo

The deceiving crab and the minnows

A crab noticed that many small fish, instead of venturing into the river, preferred to wander carefully around a boulder. The water was as clear as air and the fish swam peacefully enjoying the shade and sun.

The crab waited for the night, and when he was sure no one would see it, he went and hid under the boulder.

From that hiding place, like an ogre from his lair, he spied on the little fish and when they passed him he would catch and eat them.

It's not nice what you're doing - grumbled the boulder - Take advantage of me to kill these poor innocents.

The crab didn't even listen. Happy and content he continued to fish for the little fish, finding them delicious in flavor.

But one day, suddenly, the flood came. The river swelled, hit the boulder with great force, *which rolled into the river bed, crushing the crab under it.*

<u>Conclusions:</u>

Leonardo da Vinci: he is the genius of the Renaissance, with an immeasurable range of knowledge ranging from literature to science. Illegitimate son of the notary Piero da Vinci, he did not carry out regular study training at school - in fact he did not know Greek or Latin - but he joined, from a very young age, the Verrocchio workshop along with two other great artists : Botticelli and Perugino. His training, therefore, is not the most exemplary, but leads us to believe that, sometimes (or often), a piece of paper is worth nothing, that the greatest experience is made by touching things with your hand and not only studying theories upon theories. Five hundred years have passed since his death and this very important number pushes us, as always, to reflect, to think about how much things have changed, about how, generation after generation, we have reached the current situation, that of a world in which characters from television programs of dubious culture are raised to idols, such as the one in which the so-called "tronists" intervene. But is this really a problem? Perhaps, a single answer does not exist.

I hope the narration was enjoyable, full of ideas and questions.

If I have managed to cheer up even a few moments of your life, I am happy.

Thank you very much dear reader and listener. If you are satisfied and intrigued, you can continue the journey into the world of fantasy by reading my other books.

Thanks thanks thanks !!!

I wish you a good life!

See you soon.